A Cooking Book
Featuring
Old Bohemian Recipes

by

Marie Blaha Pearson

PublishAmerica
Baltimore

First printing

Recipes in this book were made and photographed in the author's home kitchen.
All photos in this book have been taken by the author unless otherwise noted.

ISBN: 1-4241-7785-5
PUBLISHED BY PUBLISHAMERICA, LLLP
www.publishamerica.com
Baltimore

Printed in the United States of America

In memory of

Our remarkable Bohemian ancestors who immigrated, leaving behind them in the old country, not only their villages and their loved ones, but their way of life, all for a chance of a better existence in America. They brought with them what they could carry in their own hands and hearts and souls,

And in honor

Of those, for reasons unknown, who did not immigrate, but remained behind only to experience decades of unspeakable hardships and isolation, and that only by the grace of God, somehow managed to live lives of quiet dignity and grace—I dedicate this book.

Acknowledgments

My life is so blessed to have such wonderful people in it. Nice people, encouraging people, people who care and share and trust and treat each other with respect and kindness. This cooking book or "cookery book," as they refer to recipe books in the old country, is possible because of them, my family and my friends.

There are three Czech/Slovak women who have been a tremendous help as I have gathered and collected information to be included in this book. Nancy Cerny Edwards, my cousin and childhood friend with whom I have shared many happy hours, learning needlework and crafts and discussing family history and food! Joyce Pritchard, whose abounding energy and abilities never cease to amaze me and who was the instrumental force behind our efforts to actually get to and visit our ancestral homeland and villages, the first time ever. For all her help and mentoring, I am so appreciative. Patty Blaha Henderson, my only sister, has had to endure my sometimes scattered ways of thinking and doing things, and who loves me anyway. Patty is pretty remarkable and if she wasn't already my sister, I'd want her to be.

These three, along with my husband and children, have contributed so much of themselves in so many ways to this journey I've undertaken. Perhaps the most helpful was that they recently tried, tested, and tasted most of these recipes for me and gave me their feedback. Without their thoughts, advice and wisdom, not to mention their truthfulness, it would have been much harder and not half as much fun. Dekuji.

Contents

Introduction 9

How I Came to Know Food 12

Potato Dumplings (Brambor Knedlik) 18

Cabbage and Tomato Sauce 22

Cabbage Rolls aka Pigs-in-a-Blanket 23

How to Cook a Smoked Country Ham 24

Ham Squares 25

Hungarian Gulas (Goulash) 26

Garlic Soup 28

Chicken Noodle Soup with Homemade Egg Noodles 28

The Art of Making Egg Noodles 29

Plain Noodles 31

Things That Live in the Woods 31

Hare, Rabbit, Veal or Chicken Stew 32

Wild Duck 33

Roast Venison 33

Vegetables: Cooking Them the Old Way 35

How Bohemians Make Sauerkraut—a very easy recipe 37

Succotash 38

Piccalilli 38

A Special Way with Fruit 40

Drying Fruit 41

No Sul Cinnamon Apples 41

Real Old-Fashioned Sweets 43

Ginger Snaps 43

Maly Rosol (Jelly-Filled Cookie) 44

Czechoslovakian Cookies 45

Hand-Cranked Homemade Ice Cream 46

Gingerbread 47

Angel Food Cake 47

Plain Cake 48

Grandma's Birthday Cake 49

An Old Country Easter Tradition 52

Easter Lamb Cake 53

Old Bohemian Traditional Bread and Pastries 55
Babka (Baba or Babovka) 55
Pagaèky (Biscuits with Cracklings) 56
Sweet Braided Bread (Buchta/Vanocka) 58
Walnut Bread 59
All About Making Peanut Rolls, Kolaches and Strudel 61
Dough for Peanut Rolls and Kolaches 62
Peanut Rolls 63
Peanut Roll Filling 63
Kolaches 64
Whole Poppy Seed Filling 65
Two Cheese Filling 65
Fruit Fillings 66
Nut or Poppy Seed Strudel 66
Easy Poppy Seed Filling 67
Nut Filling 67
The Old Country 68
The Village Festivities 70
Honoring our Bohemian Heritage 71
A Note from the Author 72
About the Author 73

Introduction

The name of the Czech lands Boiohaemum (Bohemia) is a derivative of the name of the Celtic tribe that conquered and colonized the territory of today's Czech Republic.

The Kingdom of Bohemia was once a major east, west, north and south trade route through the heart of Europe. As a result the Czechs and Slovaks were privileged to some of the finest foods, spices, silks and other trade goods in the world, brought to them by traders and journeymen from many other countries. Through the years as the borders of the Slavic countries changed, it became impossible to clearly identify the origin of some of the foods and recipes that developed as a result of these encounters. The Czech language, being one of the most challenging languages one ever wished to learn, must have complicated things as well. No wonder then that the Slovaks, Poles, Hungarians, Germans and other bordering neighbors of the Czechs have similar dishes with little or only slight variations in the way they were made. One only has to read the list of ingredients in other ethnic recipes to see the similarities in both the spelling and pronunciation of them.

In Southern Virginia, in our Czech and Slovak farming communities, our families too have shared their food and ways of preparing it through the past 100 years, so it is still hard to distinguish what is Bohemian from what is not. While I certainly do not claim the origin of these recipes as belonging solely to the Czechs, they are old recipes that have Czech names similar to, but not exactly like, some of the other ethnic recipes that my friends make. If I want to return to my grandma's farm, all I have to do is take one bite of a kolache or potato dumpling or homemade chicken noodle soup or any of our ethnic food that we make today and there I am, just for a moment but back there nonetheless. This happened to me a lot when I visited the family village, Gernik, in the "old country" in 2005.

I was fortunate to have had the opportunity to twice visit the former Czechoslovakia and search for our family origin in the then little Kingdom of Bohemia, now the Czech Republic. Due to emigration in the early 1800s our family moved from Bohemia into what is now Romania, where the village Gernik is located. This is where my grandfather Matyas was born and lived until he was seventeen years old. In 1903, with his parents and other relatives, he immigrated to Dinwiddie County, Virginia, where they and other

Bohemian families settled to become farmers in the tradition of their "old country," Czechoslovakia. Today, the old village remains much as it was when he left. It's a long, interesting, and historical story of how our Czech and Slovak ancestors were found living in Romania today.

Still an unfolding story, several Southern Virginia Czech and Slovaks have made family connections once again. Sadly, following World War II and especially during the communist era, our relatives lost touch with those who remained in the village. To complicate matters, our village name had changed several times through the years depending on what emperor, dictator or government claimed the territory where it is situated. We felt that it was our generation's responsibility to reconnect with the family, so in 2003, my friend Joyce Pritchard and I ventured into a search for our lost relatives.

It has been a thrilling adventure because the paths we have taken have led us to places we never dreamed possible. In search of our forefathers, we've made friends both here and abroad, which has provided even more opportunities for us to explore. Because of our pursuits, there has been a heightened interest in renewing genealogy searches among the local Czechs and Slovaks of Southern Virginia. They are re-connecting.

We now know the names of the six original and quaint Czech villages in Romania, and they have been mapped out. We have re-traced the footsteps of our ancestors from Bohemia in 1824-26, to Romania. The same footsteps that eventually led our ancestors to Virginia. We have met some of our relatives in the old country, having been guests in their homes sharing meals, drinks and friendship with them. We're learning a lot about the history and the mystery surrounding our immigrant families—stories they were hesitant to talk about when they came over. Life had been hard for them in the old country and they continued to face many difficulties upon their arrival here as well. In Southern Virginia, and elsewhere in the United States, they were free to reap the rewards of their efforts and through their sheer determination and hard work, our relatives eventually purchased and took ownership of thousands of acres of desolate farmland that needed cultivation, development and care following the American Civil War.

Our Czech and Slovak ancestors were brave, intelligent, honest and hardworking individuals. They had enough desire and ambition for peace and success to enable them to leave their native homeland for America where opportunities for them were at least equal.

Being proud of our heritage, we remain hard at work with others here and abroad to re-invent, maintain and keep alive our Czech and Slovak customs and traditions. Recipes are such a wonderful way of doing this. I hope you will enjoy reading the recipes that have been collected as well as looking at the photos and personal comments in this book. Out of many delicious Czech recipes collected, a few of our favorite and most interesting are included in this "cooking book."

How I Came to Know Food

A few years ago I ordered a book from the Internet titled *How I Came to Know Fish* by Ota Pavel. Loosely translated into English it told how he was able to learn how to fish. It was a bittersweet tale of Mr. Pavel's childhood during the occupation of Czechoslovakia in World War II. I thought it an odd title for a book but was drawn to it because of my interest in Czechoslovakia and of learning about the life and conditions families had to endure during that time period. As a child, Ota learned by observing his father and other villagers how to catch the best and biggest fish from the local ponds in the Czechoslovakian countryside. The lessons he learned valiantly as a child were the very ones that saved him and his family from starvation in later years.

After reading this little book about his sad and tragic life, I was reminded that we, as adults, are always being observed by children; that while they observe us, we are mentoring them whether we realize it at the time or not. Further, these same children will take what they see and learn from our personal interactions and behavior, and go out into the world with these images and words and deeds and—you get the picture—planted into their little minds.

I no longer think the title to Mr. Pavel's book so odd. I'm just so thankful that I, like he, had loving mentors as a child. That the things I learned in the kitchen with my relatives have served me well in my life. To use a play on the words in the title of his book: "This is how I came to know food."

Although my mother was not Czech, she might as well have been. In the early thirties when they married, Mom was engulfed into Dad's large ethnic family as if she had always been one of them. His sisters became her sisters and his brothers her brothers. That's the way it was with large immigrant families. Mom admitted that there were times when she had a hard time understanding and accepting some of the "old ways," which was typical for wives not of their husbands' origin; however, she did not let that stop her from learning how to cook their food, embroider feed sack dish towels, aprons and pillow cases, nor did it keep her from participating in most of their old family customs and traditions.

As my dad drove from our house in town to the country, finally reaching the long and dusty lane that led up to the farm, my first sensation upon arrival was one of smell. I could smell the farm. Wonderful aromas came out of the kitchen; fruit that was left ripening on the windowsills filled the air with their essence. I could smell the barns and animals and hay and the fresh air. To this very day, whenever I visit a farm, I am immediately transported back to Grandpa's, first running through the gate flanked with hollyhocks, sweet peas, and other colorful flowers, giving Grandma, who was always standing outside the screened porch waiting for us, a quick hug and not stopping until I was on the screened-in porch that led to the kitchen, slamming the door behind me unless one of my brothers was at my heels to catch it. Fruits and vegetables in various stages of ripening lined the small narrow shelves that held the screens in place. A butter churn stood tall and lonely in one corner waiting for hands, young or old—it had no preference—to perform its magic of turning cream into butter. As I made my way around that porch, I'd look to see who was sitting on the swing so that I could squeeze in with them. That was the prime seat for any family visitor, grown-up or child. Sitting in that swing was being in the center of all the activity of the day. Eventually everyone gathered in or near it whenever they needed to take a break or to just sit for a minute. As the grown-ups chatted in the background, I'd watch flies as they flew around a spiraling sticky paper flycatcher that hung from the ceiling. My goal was to not see them get caught on it but to see if they could get loose. It never happened. By the end of the day, it was always speckled with the unwanted and annoying pests that were drawn in by the different smells coming out of the kitchen, not to mention our running in and out all day.

Mom would always pitch in and help Grandma and her sisters-in-law with whatever they were doing in the kitchen. She'd also help in the gardens but not in the fields. She would not go near the farm on the cold days that they butchered but other than that, they always had a good time together. She was the first one to suggest they slip behind the barn to smoke hand-rolled cigarettes and for their girl talk. Sometimes they'd whisper or talk Pig Latin so "little ears" could not hear nor understand what they were talking about. That was the only time I found them boring. Mom had fun at their dances and socials and enjoyed the Czech food, music and gatherings but other than that, she preferred city life.

Grandma and Grandpa's was where we'd find all of our aunts, uncles and cousins, because this was where the siblings gathered each weekend. As children, we had the run of the farm in those days and we'd have so much fun playing and exploring the barns, fields and ponds. My brothers joined their male cousins for excursions in exploring the farm animals, machinery, feed and for other adventures. I loved being in the kitchen with the women, listening to them talk about weddings and funerals, new babies in the family, and how many jars of pickles, beets, snaps and other fruits and vegetables they canned and "put up" during the summer. All of this kitchen talk went on as they were preparing big family meals—and I took it all in.

The little girls in our family consisted of my baby sister Patty, my younger cousin Sissy, and me. I was the oldest. Our female relatives were inclusive and they gave us a sense of well-being, a sense of being cared for, and even as children we felt valued around them. Being the oldest, I was more interested in what was going on in the kitchen and they gave me as much time and attention as they could, considering how busy they were. Patiently they showed me how to do things properly; how to knead bread, how to stir food in a pot so it wouldn't boil over or stick to the bottom of the pan, or burn. They taught me how to peel and slice fruits and vegetables and how to watch and wait and listen to the sounds of food as it was cooking in order to know when it was ready to take up. I learned to use my eyes and ears and sense of smell, to watch for the color of perfectly browned rolls or when the tips of meringue pies were ready. I listened to the sound of chicken as it was frying so that when it was ready to take it out of the big black frying pan, I could. If my back was turned while busy doing something else, I learned, just by my sense of smell, when something was about to be overcooked. I learned to recognize when bread dough had risen enough to punch down and I eventually learned how to shape loaves of bread, though never as good then or now as Aunt Margaret's beautiful and uniform cloverleaf rolls were.

As children, we were fed after the grown-ups had eaten because as large as the table was, it could not seat everyone at the same time. Children ate last back then because it was proper. As a result, we learned a sense of patience and anticipation and control. We knew no other way of behaving because this was the custom. While our parents and family ate we'd stand tiptoe at their elbows praying that they'd save some for us. The table was piled high with all kinds of food; homemade chicken noodle soup, platters of fried chicken, ham taken from their own smoke house, and bowls of mashed potatoes, yellow from all the butter added, not to mention the gravy made from darkened pan drippings. Placed in strategic places around the table were steaming bowls of butter beans, squash, sauerkraut, and corn on the cob piled in neat rows one on top of the other and ears that had been picked just an hour earlier. Thick slices of freshly baked bread, cloverleaf rolls, kolaches and peanut rolls were passed around on platters time and time again. Large circular rounds of recently churned butter and homemade jellies and jams looked like jewels in crystal cut-glass bowls. Ice tea glasses, their bottoms white with undissolved sugar, had water droplets streaming down their sides, making wet circles on the white tablecloth. Grandma or Aunt Margaret would have to shoo us away, as they made their way back and forth from the stove to the table, refilling bowls and serving the others. After what seemed like an eternity, we were told to wash up so we'd be ready to eat when the grown-ups were through. Each of us had to be spic and span before getting to the table. The boy cousins always jumped in line first at the washstand, leaving the girls to wait for more clean water, then they'd run and sit in the first empty chairs that had been vacated by the grown-ups. It really didn't matter because we knew that once we were all seated, the "ladies" would be served first. Grandma and Aunt Margaret would sit down to eat with us, one at each end of the table, while some of the aunts who had eaten earlier began to replenish the dishes and serve us. The other ladies started the huge task of washing up all of the dishes, pots and pans that had been used in preparing food all day long.

Eventually as I grew older, I was allowed to handle the knives well enough to peel and cut out the bad specks found in the apples, pears and peaches. I was also "allowed" to dry the mounds of dishes that my mother or one of my aunts washed up; there was always an endless supply of them. My dishtowel often became as wet as the dish rag and just when I thought we were through washing up the dishes, they'd throw out the dirty dish water, walk out to the pump and get some more water, put it on the hot stove to heat up and boil, so they could finish up. My grandma had an endless supply of drying towels, all beautifully embroidered and all ready to use when a dry one was needed. When I asked when I could wash dishes instead of dry them, I was told sweetly that no one else could dry the dishes as good as me. That praise did the trick; it helped my pride and I stopped complaining. Sometimes an aunt would come to my rescue and take the towel out of my hands and say, "I'll take over, you go play."

I learned a lot in those days and I cherish the memories still. The females were my first mentors and neither they nor I even knew it at the time. Although I was learning a lot about food, what I didn't know then was that I was also learning good basic skills to take with me into adulthood. I witnessed how a cow after being milked was then given a firm "thank you" pat on her rear. Whenever I was invited to stay overnight, Aunt Margaret would take me down to the barn with her as she milked the cows, one by one. When she finished, we would take the warm liquid back to the kitchen to skim the foam from the top all the while she was explaining to me how the cream would eventually float to the top and then it could be churned into butter.

Going into the henhouse with Grandma as she gathered her eggs was considered a privilege. Children were never allowed in there because no one wanted the hens all upset. For her to take me with her was really a special event and I think it was because I was always quiet by nature. It was usually dark and dusty in there with streaks of sunlight coming in between the slats in the walls or from the doorway we left partially open. I was always amazed at how Grandma would gently but firmly reach up under a sitting hen searching for eggs. She advised me to slowly and gently reach my hand confidently under them while looking at them, letting them know who was boss. Believe me, I never took my eyes off them. It took some practice but eventually, I got pretty good at it. To be honest, I preferred to either shoo them away or take the eggs out of empty nests. I was not as sure of myself as she was. Not being afraid of the chickens didn't hold true about the roosters. Grandma often reminded me that outside, they were the boss and to watch out for them, which I did. They even looked mean.

Sometimes Aunt Margaret would let Sissy and me help her feed the chickens. She would take handfuls of dried corn out of her bucket and holding up the hem of our dresses she'd make a place to hold it so that we'd have our own feed to scatter about. She told us we had to call them to us by saying, "Here, chick, chick; here, chick, chick," and it always worked because they'd come running up to us as we quickly threw out handfuls of that corn for them.

Once, after I persisted and nagged long enough, Aunt Margaret gave in and let me try to churn butter. What she knew that I didn't know and had to learn the hard way was that it was hard work. It didn't take me long until it felt like my arms were going to break off. After leaving me alone for a few minutes, she came along and took over this job for me. Even though I was a bother to her about this, she gave me the credit for making it turn into real butter. That's how nice she was.

My childhood memories are sweet; of feeling cherished and included into a woman's world. I remember how safe and secure I felt being among good, busy and loving women. I felt happy to be rewarded by the "oohs and awws" when my own little pan of hot rolls came out of the oven, unshapely and uneven but warm and brown and delicious nonetheless. I enjoyed hearing the "men folks" tease me, saying how a little girl could not possibly have made anything that tasted that good. I give credit to these early models in my life, as being responsible for my love of cooking today and for the sweet memories I have of them.

Although we were "city slickers," Mom, having learned the Czech way of making their favorite recipes, continued to encourage my sister Patty and me to stay in the kitchen with her to see how things were made. Through the years we've learned to love and respect this food and though we grumble sometimes about how time-consuming the dishes are to make, we never let a holiday pass without making most, if not all, of the holiday recipes in this book. Mom instilled into our very souls how important it is to keep family traditions alive by continuing to make these dishes even when the old folks were gone and the visits to the country stopped. Today they are implanted in our minds and it just wouldn't be Thanksgiving or Christmas without some of this food on our tables.

Patty and I often give each other "the look" when one of our children asks us how we make potato dumplings, one of the most time-consuming of all these recipes. We tell them the same thing our mother told us: "potatoes, flour, salt and eggs, but you need to come over and watch me make them, it's the best way to learn."

To be fair, in those days, that was the best advice we could give them, because it is a recipe that really helps when you can see it being made rather than trying it alone the first time. But times have changed and so has my advice. It took me a long time, even after watching Mom make them, to consistently make decent batches. It took practice and experience but now it is a lot easier for me to explain the way this recipe and other Czech dishes are made since I've discovered how useful digital cameras and computers are. With the help of this technology, the "now generation" who wants to make these potato dumplings can look at the recipe, follow the step-by-step directions, see the illustrated photos, and become an expert in making them the very first time. In fact, anyone who wants to learn Bohemian cookery from scratch can do this too.

Part of the complexity of making potato dumplings is that it can be time-consuming and messy. This did not seem to be a problem with our grandparents on the farm because usually there were at least two, and maybe more, inter-generational women in the family who shared kitchen chores back then. Today, we usually find ourselves alone in the kitchen to do all of the cooking and cleaning up because everyone else is busy with other responsibilities. There are several easier ways that will help when making some of these recipes but the real old-fashioned ways are given first. Hopefully the notes and hints, along with the step-by-step directions and photos, will serve as helpful shortcuts, especially for the next generation of Bohemian cooks, our sons and daughters and their children.

Potato Dumplings (Brambor Knedlik)

"Come over and watch me make then, it's the best way to learn"

A form of this ethnic recipe for potato dumplings came to America with our immigrant grandparents early in the 1900s from Czechoslovakia. As agrarians who raised their own food, potatoes were a staple food source in many kitchens because they were plentiful. Potatoes were a food source that was economical and one that was able to quickly fill up hungry stomachs of the men, women and children who worked the land. Similar recipes are found among other Eastern European ethnic groups because by combining potatoes with flour, eggs and salt, housewives were assured of providing healthy, substantial, and good-tasting food at mealtimes. When our ancestral grandmothers and their mothers before them made potato dumplings they knew two things: one, that this was a vegetable that could be stretched with other ingredients if need be, and two, that leftovers, if any, would be just as good when reheated and served later as it was when they were originally made.

The Czechs typically spooned a hearty cabbage and tomato sauce over the dumplings, because by themselves they tend to be somewhat bland. Later the leftovers, when thinly sliced and sautéed in butter, created a different and delicious side dish. Nothing was ever wasted by these hardworking, self-sufficient and frugal Bohemians, be it food or other goods.

There are three steps in making Potato Dumplings.
First: Mixing
Second: Boiling
Third: Frying

Ingredients:

Potatoes (the number of people to feed determines the number of pounds of potatoes. Example: 10 pounds of potatoes yields 50 to 60 dumplings.)
All-purpose flour (to be safe, have on hand equal amounts of flour as potatoes. Example: 5 pounds of potatoes and 5 pounds of flour.)
2 eggs for each batch
2 Tbsp. salt (more as needed)
Crisco (for frying)

Step 1. Clean unpeeled potatoes then boil until soft. Cool long enough to handle, then peel. Mash the potatoes before they are completely cold. Some small lumps are desired.
Step 2. When ready to start making the dumplings, put a large pan of salted water over medium heat and bring to a boil. Once boiling, turn down the heat and allow the water to simmer while making the dumplings.
Step 3. Place a generous amount of flour on a flat surface forming a ring. Make a large well in the center of the ring.
Step 4. Place the mashed potatoes into the center of the well. Make an indentation in the potatoes and add the eggs and salt.

Step 5. Using your hands, begin blending the flour from the ring into the potato and egg mixture until all is well incorporated. Add more flour as the kneading process requires.

(This step can be messy, and it takes time, but it can be relaxing particularly if you like to work with dough. Also, it may help at this point to divide the potato/dough into two sections, working half at a time, especially if you are using lots of potatoes in order to make a lot of dumplings.)

Step 6. As the dough begins to hold its shape, continue adding flour and kneading until a firm log begins to form. Make sure the log is firm enough so that when it is cut and dropped into boiling water, it will hold its shape. You will more than likely make more than one log if you use more than a couple pounds of potatoes.

(If you have separated your potato dough in half, now is the time to complete the second half, following step six, before continuing the recipe.)

Step 7. Once each log is formed, cut it into one-inch-thick dumplings. Meanwhile turn the pan of simmering water up so that a medium boil can be reached and maintained.

Step 8. Drop the dumplings into the pan of boiling water one at a time. Cover the pot and cook the dumplings for 10 to 12 minutes. Stir them a couple of times while boiling to make sure they do not stick to the bottom of the pan. The dumplings will sink to the bottom at first but rise up and float when they are done. Once the dumplings have risen to the top of the boiling water, remove them with a slotted spoon and place them on absorbent towels. Repeat until all the dumplings have been boiled.

Step 9. Place a generous spoonful of Crisco into a large skillet and melt over medium heat. Fry each dumpling until slightly brown. Some crusts may form when turning the dumplings over, but this is the good part. This process of frying is mainly to "dry them out" so they are not slick; remember they were already cooked through by being boiled. As each batch is fried, it may be necessary to add more shortening to the pan. Salt lightly when they are removed from the frying pan. Serve hot with a cabbage and tomato sauce. When carefully wrapped, these dumplings freeze nicely.

It takes a while to knead this dough once all the ingredients have been added. As I get into the rhythm of the kneading, the pushing and pulling, the same thing over and over waiting for it to form just right, my mind wanders back to the farm where I've seen my grandma and aunts knead dough hundreds of times. I see the big black cast-iron stove that was in the kitchen before they got electricity. It had a wood box beside it filled with short cuts of wood that had been perfectly chopped to fit into it. I can still see the red blazing logs and embers and feel the heat when the door was opened. I see pots boiling on that iron stove with steam rising above and the wonderful aromas of fresh vegetables seeping out. I think about the poetry of movement as my aunt or grandma juggled the pots around, finding just the right spot for the perfect cooking temperature that certain foods needed.

Since this has always been such a nourishing activity for me, I tend to think that every woman needs to knead now and then, just for the pure therapy of it.

One is never too young to make this recipe. My granddaughter McKenzie Adams at age six is giving it a try.

Some tips to think about when making potato dumplings.

Begin this recipe early in the day, before you are tired. The smaller the batch, the easier this recipe is to make.

Peel potatoes before boiling.

Mash the potatoes while they're still warm, then let cool enough to handle.

Place the flour into a large pan with sides before making the well and indentations. (A cookie baking pan works well for this).

21

When working the flour into dough, do not stop kneading if the batch is still sticky or fails to hold its shape. Although you may think that there is enough flour worked in, there may not be; keep adding more until the log is solid.

For best results, cut the dumplings and place in boiling water as soon as the logs become firm. They don't wait well.

Flour the blade of the knife when cutting the dumplings.

Cabbage and Tomato Sauce

1 medium head of cabbage, cleaned, cored and chopped
2 tsp. salt
2 No.2 cans of tomatoes
4 Tbsp. butter
4 Tbsp. flour

Place chopped cabbage into a large pot of salted boiling water. Cook slowly until tender. When the cabbage is tender and the liquid has been reduced, add tomatoes and continue cooking for another half hour.

Once the cabbage and tomatoes have finished cooking, make a blonde roux*. Add the roux to the mixture. Continue cooking over low heat until the mixture thickens slightly. Stir often to prevent sticking. Serve by spooning over Czech Potato Dumplings.

*Blonde Roux: (Roux is made by using equal amounts of butter and flour.) Over medium heat, melt butter in a small frying pan. Add flour and stir until the flour is completely absorbed by the butter. Continue stirring a few minutes allowing it to burn off the flour taste, but removing it from the heat before it turns brown in color.

Cabbage Rolls
aka Pigs-in-a-Blanket

It takes a while for some people to acquire a taste for this dish, especially non-Czech spouses and children. It's because it does not give off the best aroma when cooking, and just the name "sauerkraut" to some is a big turn-off. But if you can ever get them to taste it more than once, they're hooked forever because it is mighty good. Some of my Polish and Slovak friends add a little tomato sauce, which to them enhances the flavor and the looks of this dish.

1 lb. ground beef
½ lb. ground pork
½ cup cooked rice
½ tsp. salt
Dash of pepper
1 head of cabbage
1 qt. sauerkraut (homemade if possible)

Core cabbage and steam until the leaves are pliable enough to be peeled from the head. Set aside. Combine beef, pork, rice, salt, pepper, mixing well. Place a heaping tablespoon of this mixture into the center of each cabbage leaf; fold leaf over meat mixture then roll securely. Place a layer of sauerkraut into the bottom of a heavy pan or baking dish. Place cabbage rolls on top of the layer. Continue alternating sauerkraut and cabbage rolls, then cover with warm water. Simmer over medium heat for two hours. (If preferred, it could be baked at 350 degrees for the same amount of time.) At the end of the allotted time, whether cooked on top of the stove or baked, cut into one of the cabbage rolls to make sure that the meat has been thoroughly cooked. If not, continue cooking another ½ hour at a time until done. Serve while hot.

How to Cook a Smoked Country Ham

Once in Virginia our Bohemian families learned that peanut-fed hogs produced the best hams they ever tasted. They quickly learned from their neighbors how they smoked their Virginia hams and the results were outstanding. As kids, we were never allowed to open the door to the smokehouse, but Aunt Margaret or Grandma would let me peek in if one of them went out there for anything. People today say they don't much care for "salty ham." I'm always amazed when I hear that because I never knew a time when I didn't like it. While this particular method of smoking hams did not come from Old Bohemia, our Old Bohemians adopted it from some Old Virginians.

There are two accepted ways of cooking a smoked ham: on top of the stove by boiling it, or placed in the oven to bake. I see no difference in the taste no matter which method I use so I usually bake it overnight so that the next morning, I can skin and de-bone it while it's still warm. That frees up my oven for other things during the day. Either way the ham must be soaked all day or all night. When ready to cook the ham, remove it from the water, wash it in warm water, using a stiff brush to remove the mold and pepper.

To boil: Place the ham in a large pot and cover with water. Bring it to a boil and let it cook slowly for several hours until the bone wiggles freely. Remove the ham from the water; skin and de-bone when cool enough to handle.

To bake: After washing and brushing away the mold and pepper, completely wrap the ham in thick foil. Before sealing, pour 6 cups of water into the bottom of the foil. Place the ham in a large roasting pan and place in a 400-degree preheated oven for 20 minutes. Turn the oven off. After 3 hours turn the oven on again and let temperature reach 400 degrees, bake for another 20 minutes. Turn the oven off and do not open the door again for at least 8 hours. Remove from oven, unwrap, trim off the skin and de-bone.

Ham Squares

This is another recipe that brings back memories for me. Mom always made it for Easter dinner, using some of the country ham. Dad's job was to grind the ham for Mom. I would pester him until he let me try to turn the handle of the old food grinder he had screwed onto the wooden kitchen table. It didn't take me long to realize that I was too small and not strong enough to turn the handle all the way around by myself. To comfort me, Dad would hand me the bowl to hold under the lip of the grinder as the meat poured out. After a few times of this, I lost interest in trying to do it. I still have that grinder today and although I never use it, I can't seem to get rid of it either. Using my food processor makes more sense to me.

Grandma and Aunt Margaret used left-over country ham to make this casserole and that is the secret of its success. Otherwise it's just a little too bland. I asked my cousins if they had the old recipe but none of them could come up with a copy. We all agreed on the ingredients if not the methods our parents used because some of my aunts layered the ham and noodles in the casserole dish, while others mixed it all up together. Wide store-bought egg noodles were generally used unless they felt really ambitious and made their own. Being somewhat bland I add some dry mustard to the custard because I think it gives this dish the little boost it needs. This then, is the "re-invention" of this recipe by consensus.

4 cups of salty ham, ground
6 eggs (well-beaten)
3 cups cream
3 Tbsp. flour
I tsp. salt
½ tsp. pepper
2 Tbsp. dry mustard
1 (12 oz.) package extra-wide egg noodles (cooked and drained)

Layer the noodles and ham into a square buttered casserole dish. Beat eggs, milk, flour and mustard together; add salt and pepper. Pour egg custard mixture over the layers of ham and noodles until the ham and noodles are completely covered. Place foil on top of casserole and bake in a preheated 375-degree oven for 45 minutes or until the center is set. (This can be determined by inserting the tip of a knife into the center; if it comes out clean the casserole is ready.) Remove the foil during the last 5 minutes of baking, allowing the casserole to brown slightly. Let stand about 5 minutes before cutting into squares; serve warm.

Hungarian Gulas (Goulash)

Nowhere can one find an "official" recipe for Hungarian goulash. People made it many different ways according to their own traditions and taste. Perhaps because it was known as "country food" it took a while before it began to show up on the menus of upscale restaurants in Prague and Vienna. Once it gained favor in the ritzy hotels in those beautiful cities it was no longer considered peasant food but became a poplar and desirable main course for their diners.

Paprika is the spice that is always found in ethnic goulash. It is made from red peppers that have been dried and ground into a fine powder. As a garnish it is basically tasteless, but when used in recipes such as this, it gives a stronger and different taste to food. So much is used in "real" Hungarian gulas that everything takes on the deep red color. When served over a heaping plate of noodles it makes both an attractive and delicious main meal.

Goulash is a dish that can be made early in the day, put into a pot on the stove, and left alone to simmer until dinnertime. In fact, the longer it cooks, the more tender the meat becomes. It is also a great way to use the tougher cuts of beef because the meat breaks down when cooked long and slow. My mom made it without much paprika, just enough to satisfy the Bohemian gods, no garlic and no beer—but she still called it goulash. She also added chunks of diced potatoes and onions to the meat and let it cook all afternoon. When she served it, usually with hot biscuits and honey, we devoured it.

2 lbs. beef or pot roast meat cut into chunks
2 Tbsp. oil
2 medium onions, chopped coarsely
2 tsp. crushed garlic
¼ cup paprika
1 tsp. salt
½ tsp. ground black pepper
1 bottle of (Pilsner) beer or homebrew
1 tsp. marjoram
1 tsp. caraway seeds
2 bay leaves
4 large potatoes, cut into medium-size chunks
Water to cover

Heat a heavy pot with oil until very hot. Sear the meat on all sides. Once the meat is nicely browned, add onions, cooking until they are brown and caramelized. To this add the garlic, a bottle of beer, and remaining spices. Blend well. Cover with water and let it cook for at least 1½ to 2 hours or until the meat is tender. Serve over egg noodles unless chunks of potatoes have been added.

Garlic Soup

This is a great recipe to serve on a cold winter's night or to use if one is not feeling well. It produces a beautiful clear broth. Not only does it provide light nourishment, it is delicious as well. It's easy to make and the recipe is easily adjusted depending on how many people there are to feed.

½ stick butter
½ cup diced celery (include leaves)
4 Tbsp. garlic, minced
1 cup thinly sliced onions
2 qts. chicken broth
Salt and pepper to taste

Sauté onions and celery in butter until they are transparent. Add garlic. Do not let them brown.

Add chicken broth, salt, and pepper. Bring soup to a rapid boil. Turn the heat down and allow the soup to simmer until ready to serve. It can be served at once or allowed to simmer longer. Makes 4–6 servings.

Chicken Noodle Soup with Homemade Egg Noodles

Bohemians love their soup and it is almost always served as the first course in their households. Chicken soup seems to be preferred but sometimes rice is added instead of noodles. This is a wonderful basic soup recipe that is so versatile that chicken and dumplings, chicken and rice or chicken and noodle soup can all be made using it. Our all-time favorite is this one.

1 whole chicken
Water to cover
1 Tbsp. salt
¼ tsp. pepper
1 onion diced
1 carrot diced
1 stalk of celery diced
1 bay leaf
Homemade egg noodles (see recipe below)

Cover the whole chicken with water; add salt and pepper. Boil until the meat starts to pull away from the bones. Reserve the broth. Remove the chicken from the liquid and allow it to cool. Take away the meat from the bones and shred or cut into bite-size pieces.

To the soup broth, add the cut-up chicken, diced vegetables, seasonings, and additional water if needed. Bring to a boil and allow the soup to simmer until the vegetables are tender. Next, add homemade egg noodles and boil for about 4 or 5 minutes longer. Serve hot.

The Art of Making Egg Noodles

(This procedure takes a little time, practice and patience, but according to our babushkas, this is the old way, and the only way, to make noodles.)

There is an art in making egg noodles that is as old as time and that is in jeopardy of becoming lost. To be still and just watch our Bohemian grandmas make egg noodles was like watching poetry in motion. The skill in making this dough, the swiftness of using both of their hands in unison and the final production of this craft was awesome to see.

To our babushkas, making egg noodles in this tradition was nothing special, but when their old arthritic hands began working together, blending the eggs and flour into a rich, delicious and colorful dough, it was indeed special. The dough being formed took on the rich color of the egg yolks while the oil gave it a beautiful shiny sheen; and it all appeared in a certain rhythm, a quiet heartbeat, that denied one from taking their eyes away while it was happening.

The secret of making egg noodles this way is that you must have dexterity and coordination. Both hands must be used at the same time; one making circular strokes, the other linear ones. Being able to use both hands differently and in unison is not as difficult as it seems but it does take concentration, and for some like me, practice. Of course, there's nothing wrong in making these noodles the regular way, (see recipe below) either. It's just that mixers, dough hooks and using fewer eggs is not the traditional way.

Old recipes should be more than collector's items and to make this happen, we need to make sure that our modern kitchen equipment that makes things easier for us, does not take make our traditional ways become a lost art. If taste, texture and tradition are the criteria for saving old heritage recipes, this is one that should be kept.

8 egg yolks
4 or more cups all-purpose flour
Pinch of salt
2 Tbsp. oil

Make a well in the flour into which you place the egg yolks and salt. Gently break the yolks by stirring them together in a circular motion with the first two fingers of your dominant hand. Add the oil and salt. Continue stirring in this way while using the first two fingers of your other hand to brush the flour from the inside of the well gently into the yolk mixture. Continue stirring and adding flour in this manner until the eggs and oil can no longer absorb any more flour.

Once the dough is formed, turn out and knead this mixture on a lightly floured board until it is smooth and silky. Cover and let it rest a few minutes then divide it into four sections. (Keep each section covered until ready to roll out.) Working with one section at a time, roll the dough out very thin. Cut into strips. Continue rolling and cutting the remaining sections of dough until all the noodles are made. These rich and delicious noodles may be dried and stored if not used immediately.

Plain Noodles

There is another way to make homemade noodles that is much easier and that is really good. To make plain noodles, omit the oil; mix together

2 eggs
A pinch of salt
2 cups of flour
Water (added 2 tablespoons at a time)

Roll out very thin and cut into strips. Use immediately or allow to dry and store.

Things That Live in the Woods

Czechoslovakia is a country that is landlocked on all sides but is not lacking beautiful rivers, streams, and ponds that attract all of God's creatures, including man. Hunting and fishing was more than a sport or a pleasurable pastime for the men in the old country; it was a necessity. Our ancestors, who lived in small villages surrounded by mountains and forests and woodlands, not only loved to hunt, they needed to put meat on their tables. Fishing was also a great opportunity for men to get their bragging rights and to help fill their cold-room as well. Carp grew quite large in public and private ponds in the old country and men and boys spent many hours on the shores of them trying to outwit these fish. Goose feathers, tied on the end of a fishing line was the choice lure while in the kitchen it was their wives' useful pastry brush.

During the depression in Virginia and elsewhere in the states, wild game was also a welcome addition in most kitchens. I'm not sure when hunting became more of a sport than a necessity, but I can't recall any Czech or Slovak man, then or now, who doesn't love to hunt and fish, and who can't tell you with pride in his voice, how many, how big and how difficult the hunt was in getting their trophies.

It seems to me that times have changed. In the past, men would go out hunting or fishing and bring home whatever their skill or luck allowed. Returning home, they expected their mothers, wives or daughters to clean and cook it, which they did. It has taken several generations, but this is changing. Today, when they go hunting and fishing, they field dress their game, clean their fish on the spot, and bring it home to fine-tune it for the freezer or frying pan. Then, when it's ready for the pot, they usually do the cooking themselves. I love to hear them discuss their recipes. Each has a secret ingredient or special method that makes it "really delicious." We've come a long way and so have our men.

Hare, Rabbit, Veal or Chicken Stew

Bohemian cooking does not often call for spices and herbs to be used in their recipes. Usually dumplings, sweet or savory, are added instead. This is one of a few recipes where this is the exception.

2 oz. butter
2-3 lbs. (depending on the amount of bone) of hare or rabbit joints, stewing veal or chicken joints
2 coarsely chopped onions
4 cloves garlic, chopped finely
4 potatoes, peeled and diced
3 ¾ cups water
3 generous tablespoons red or white wine vinegar

2 bay leaves
Salt and pepper to taste
15 fresh, roughly chopped sage leaves, or 1 Tbsp. dried sage

Sauté the onions and garlic in butter in a heavy skillet until they are transparent. Add the meat and sear until lightly browned. Next add the potatoes, water, vinegar, bay leaves and remaining seasoning. Bring the pot to a boil, cover it and simmer gently for 1 to 1½ hours or till the meat is tender and ready to fall from the bones. Add the sage and continue to cook for several minutes. Before serving, remove the bones and gristle from the stew.

Wild Duck

Wild duck should be served very rare. When the duck has been dressed and cleaned, stuff with sliced apple or onion. Sprinkle with salt, pepper and put two thin slices of bacon on the breast. Bake for 25 minutes in a very hot oven. It will produce a lot of grease as it bakes. Baste often, using the fat in the pan. Note: Basting with apple juice enhances the flavor and helps cut the grease. Be advised: most wild ducks are smaller than they appear when they are full of feathers, so I wouldn't expect to serve a lot of people with just one duck.

Roast Venison

Between 1885 and 1910, about the same time our ancestors were arriving in the United States, according to my research, there were only about 500,000 deer left in all of America. Bison vanished and other big-game animals were on the brink of extinction. As a result, President Teddy Roosevelt intervened and with the help of hunt club members, licensing, and other conservation methods he put into place, the populations of not only deer but all of the other big game increased rapidly. By 1920, according to the Department of Interior, the deer populations in the national forests increased five-fold.

Wild game has probably kept millions of our forefathers both in America as well as in the old country from starvation. Like goulash, there is no "official recipe" for venison, as most people who cook it have their own special touch and list of ingredients that makes it really delicious. This is a good basic recipe that is easily adjusted to suit the "chef's" own personal taste. Having had all the fat trimmed away, herbs and spices are used to add flavor.

Venison, loin or cut of choice
½ cup dry red wine
¼ cup olive oil
1 Tbsp. salt
1 Tbsp. crushed rosemary
1 Tbsp. dried parsley
½ tsp. black pepper
¼ tsp. cloves
Several cloves of garlic
1 cup sliced carrots
1 cup sliced onions
1 cup diced celery
2 cups water
6 slices of bacon

Make a marinade out of the wine, oil, herbs and spices. Mix together. (The marinade can easily be doubled or tripled depending on the size of the roast.) Cut a few slits in the meat with a sharp knife and push cloves of garlic into the slits. Add the venison to the marinade and place in the refrigerator overnight. The next day, remove the roast from the marinade and place in a roasting pan. Place the bacon strips over the meat. Add carrots, onions, celery, water and the remaining marinade. Cover and place in a 400-degree oven for 20 minutes. Reduce the heat to 350 degrees and cook 10 to 15 minutes per pound. Baste with the pan drippings about every 15 to 20 minutes until done. Strain the pan drippings to make gravy.

Vegetables: Cooking Them the Old Way

Maud E. Cooke in her 1902 cookbook titled *20th Century Cook Book* tells how vegetables were prepared at this time in our history. I doubt that our immigrant relatives even owned a cookbook when they first came to this country, rather they brought with them the knowledge of preparing foods in the way they learned from their forefathers (or foremothers.) I do think though that this is an example of the way most of them prepared some of their vegetables.

Cauliflower, Boiled—Pick off outer leaves and cut off the stem, wash well in cold water, tie up in a thin cloth and stand in a kettle of boiling water. Add a little salt, and cover; let cook until tender. Lift carefully from the water, take off the cloth. Pick apart; put in a dish and pour melted butter over it. Dredge with pepper.

Boiled Peas—To half a peck allow a breakfast cupful of water; 1 ounce of butter, 1 large lump of loaf sugar, a pinch of salt and a sprig of mint. Serve with the liquor. The mint can be omitted if it is not liked.

String Beans—String beans require 2 hours to cook; cut them in bits first, stringing carefully. At the end of the first hour a teaspoonful of salt to each quart of beans should be added. After they are done all the water should be poured off, and to the beans should be added 1 tablespoonful of butter and 4 tablespoonfuls of boiling water. Return to the fire for 3 minutes and serve.

Turnips—Turnips boiled with their jackets on are of better flavor and less watery. A small bit of sugar added while the vegetable is boiling corrects the bitterness often found in them. Cut up and mash with pepper, butter and salt.

Spinach, Plain—Spinach should be cooked so as to retain its bright, green color, and not sent to the table, as it so often is, a dull brown. To keep its fresh green color leave the kettle, in which it is cooking, uncovered. This course may be pursued with any other vegetable where it is desirable to retain the green color, like Brussels sprouts and asparagus. Wash the spinach very thoroughly in several waters, as insects and sand are to be found in it. Drain and cook 15 or 20 minutes in boiling salted water; skim if necessary. Take up, drain and press well. Chop fine and put in a saucepan with a piece of butter and a little pepper. Stir it over the fire until quite dry. Turn into a vegetable dish; round it up. Slice hard-boiled eggs over the top. Pass vinegar around with it.

Baked Winter Squash—Boil or steam, mash and let get cold, then beat up light with 1 tablespoonful melted butter, 2 raw eggs, 3 tablespoonfuls milk; pepper and salt to taste. Put in buttered bake dish, sift dry crumbs over the top and bake in a quick oven.

Boiled Beets—Wash the beets carefully, and do not cut off the roots, for by so doing the juices escape and the color is spoiled. Boil them several hours; the time varies according to the age and season. When young and small they require about an hour. When they are done, pour off the hot water and cover them with cold water. Rub off the skin; cut them in rather thin slices and season with plenty of fresh butter, salt and pepper, and, if you like, a tablespoonful or more vinegar. Keep some of the nicest to slice cold in vinegar for pickles.

Ms. Cooke's cookbook is a rare find and makes interesting reading for food lovers. An Internet search revealed that there are still a very few copies out there.

How Bohemians Make Sauerkraut—
a very easy recipe

Sauerkraut is not a child's dish. It took all of us years to acquire a taste for this wonderful side dish. When Mom made it at home, I would only wonder how in this world anyone could eat anything that smelled so bad. I can't remember when this changed in me but somewhere along the way I acquired a taste for it and I can eat it right out of the jar today. It's that good. My mom and dad worked in the kitchen as a team and Dad's job was to chop the cabbage while Mom sterilized the jars and lids, getting everything else ready for the canning. I know they would have enjoyed the use of a food processor and other kitchen tools we have available today.

1 firm head of cabbage
Salt
Sugar
Quart Mason jars
1 piece lids and rubber rings

Wash and core the cabbage; chop into fine shreds. Pack tightly into quart Mason jars. Place 1 teaspoon salt and 1 teaspoon sugar on the top of the cabbage in each jar. Cover cabbage with boiling water. Seal jars with lids. Store in a cool place for six weeks or longer before using. It will begin to discolor during this time, but it's to be expected and desired.

Succotash

It is so easy to make succotash. Depending on how many family, visitors or field hands the women had to feed determined how many ears of corn and pounds of butter beans they needed to make this wonderful side dish.

Corn on the cob (boiled)
Butterbeans (left over or pre-cooked)
Salt & pepper to taste
Cream
Flour

Scrape the kernels and milk off of the cobs of boiled corn. Add an equal amount of butterbeans and cook together in butter. Dust with flour and add light cream. Season with salt and pepper. Serve while hot.

Piccalilli

This is a word I've always loved. It just rolls out of my mouth in a smile. I loved to come home when Mom was making this relish and smell the sweet strong aroma of vinegar that permeated the entire house. I would barely taste it, but as I grew up I learned to savor this wonderful condiment. The fact that Czech food rarely has herbs and spices added gives us a clue that piccalilli has East Indies origins, but Slavic cooks, being the frugal people they are, used up their end-of-season vegetables by making this ancient and delicious relish as well.

1 quart chopped cabbage
1 quart chopped green tomatoes
2 red bell peppers, finely chopped
3 green bell peppers, finely chopped
2 cups celery, finely chopped

2 large mild onions, chopped
¼ cup salt
¼ cup mustard seed
2 Tbsp. celery seed
1 ½ tsp. turmeric
2 cups packed brown sugar
2 cups cider vinegar
1 ½ cups water

Mix the chopped vegetables together with the salt and let sit overnight. The next morning drain and press out the liquid that formed. Add the vinegar and sugar. Put the spices together in a bag made from cheesecloth and tie with a string. Add it to the mixture. Bring to a boil and simmer until it is clear and slightly thickened (about five minutes.)

Pour the relish into sterilized and hot canning jars. Wipe rims well and seal with new lids and sterilized rings. Allow to cool then store upright in a cool, dark and dry place. Refrigerate after opening.

Note: Before Teflon pots and pans, only stainless steel or enamel pans were recommended because the acid in this recipe would discolor aluminum pans. Today, that's not as big of a problem, but worth mentioning just in case.

A Special Way with Fruit

Fruit trees were always plentiful on the farms of Czech and Slovak immigrants. Growing fruit was a natural part of their culture in the old country and Virginia provided them with just the right soil and growing conditions to continue this tradition. No decent Bohemian farm would be without their fruit trees, growing in neat rows in uncultivated fields. Other than the usual apples, peaches, cherries and plums, they grew other fruits such as persimmons, grapes, blueberries and strawberries. During summer canning season, the women worked very hard to put up jars of canned fruits and vegetables for the winter. They took pride in the final products and talked about how many jars of this or that they had canned. The kitchen was a place to stay away from unless you wanted something to do. Canning was hard work in a hot kitchen and idle hands were not tolerated.

Toward the end of the growing season, we kids were often sent out to pick up the apples that had fallen under the trees. Wormholes and small rotten specks could be cut away so we had no excuse to come back empty-handed. Picking them off the tree was not allowed because we were told those on the ground would "go bad" if they were not gathered timely. "Those on the tree may not be quite ripe," our grown-ups said. Although we could not pick them, that did not stop us, especially the boys, from jumping up to grab the limbs and shaking them as hard as we could to help the fruit fall "accidentally." As city slickers, we thought this was fun and often filled the buckets lickety-split.

Later in the summer, the fruit was often smaller and used for drying rather than canning. Drying fruit, rather than canning, was easier because it did not require all the boiling pots of water for hot jars and other things that regular canning did.

Drying Fruit

Wash, peel, core and cut into even slices about three dozen apples or peaches. Place slices on shallow sheet pans so the slices do not touch each other. Place the pans into the oven at (110–150 degrees) and leave for six hours. You will need to turn them at least twice during those six hours. They can be left overnight. To test to see if they are ready, make sure when squeezed there is no moisture. The outside of the dried fruit should be dry but soft and pliable on the inside. Do not let the fruit become brittle or hard. After you are satisfied that they are ready, put the dried fruit in a container and cover loosely. For the next four or five days, pour the fruit back and forth from bowl to bowl. This will condition it. After the fifth day, store in pint jars and tie brown paper over the tops. This makes enough for four pies.

No Sul Cinnamon Apples

Here is an apple story I will tell on myself even though I can't believe I did this. When I was on my mission trip staying at Bet'lem, the home for handicapped adults in the Czech Republic, our group was asked to prepare them a typical American meal. On our last day there, my friend Ruth and I agreed to do this. Counting patients, staff, and our group we figured on twenty people. Meanwhile while Ruth and I were to prepare the lunch, the other three in our group decided they would finish up the painting and other small jobs that we had started during our week at the home. Everyone was happy with everything we had done for them and we were all feeling the satisfaction and glow one often gets from volunteerism—being there had been a wonderful experience for all of us.

"Cook" and her helper wanted to take that afternoon off so they gladly showed us around their kitchen. (None of us could speak or understand the other's language mind you, but we felt fairly well orientated.) Not fully equipped as you might guess, the kitchen had two ovens, a cook top, familiar-looking utensils, salt, sugar, and flour—all sitting side by side in look-alike uncovered bowls, but all well marked in Czech. After discovering what was locally available, our "typical American Meal" menu was to be a fresh tossed salad, oven-fried chicken, oven-fried cinnamon apples, and parsley potatoes. We thought this was a reasonable menu but little did we know what a disaster that meal would turn out to be. This is what we learned later.

First, we should never have assumed that any good Czech would prefer a light salad as a first course, rather than their usual hearty soup.

Second, five chickens requested from the village butcher is not enough to feed twenty hungry Czechs. Furthermore, five small chickens should be cut very carefully with a sharp instrument, not an old dull knife. Ruth and I quickly told our group that they were not hungry and would not be having any lunch that day. Five extra pieces of chicken looked good to us and was extremely necessary.

Third, frugal Czech cooks do not peel their apples. Wasteful. When sugar and salt are in identical uncovered bowls, it's not too difficult to mistake the salt for sugar. Cinnamon apples require lots of sugar—if salt is used in its place it really ruins the taste.

Next, lunch is expected to be at 12 noon sharp when cook rings the bell. If the bell is not rung, everyone shows up anyway wanting their food— waiting for another pan of apples to cook is not a good thing.

Finally, when "cook" returns to her kitchen and finds it full of greasy, baked-on sticky pans, piled-up dishes that have not found their resting place, and gives you "her look," one smiles sweetly and leaves the kitchen quickly when she throws her head toward the exit door. We decided that not understanding the Czech language that day "was a good thing."

P.S.—Ruth's potatoes tasted mighty good.

Bohemain Baking

Real Old-Fashioned Sweets
Ginger Snaps

In the old days, women hardly finished one meal before it was time to begin another. Being in the kitchen before sunup until after sundown was a normal way of life for them. Not only did they prepare large meals for their tired and hardworking families, they fed the chickens, milked the cows, churned butter, and scooted the barn cats and yard dogs out of the way. Also, they gathered eggs, made clothes for the family, quilts for the beds, and did their housework, all while taking care of the little ones who ran underfoot.

Generally, special-occasion baking such as birthday cakes, holiday breads, and company cooking was done on Saturdays when women did not work in the fields as they often did during the week. During the growing and harvesting seasons, it frequently took everyone in the family to work outside in order to get their crops to market on time. For example, when it was time to hoe peanuts both the women and the children were needed in the fields to dig up the stubborn wire-grass roots that loved to grow close and choke out the tender plants. Only "Grandma" remained behind during those times to tend to the cooking, gardens and babies.

This is an old cookie recipe with a real old-fashioned taste. Not only that, it's easy to make and the house smells heavenly while they're baking. For those who worked so hard, coming home for a short rest and finding a big plate of gingersnaps and a glass of cold milk waiting for them was a special treat.

1 cup molasses
A piece of shortening the size of an egg*
2/3 tsp. soda
1 tsp. ginger
Pinch of salt
Flour (about 2 or more cups)

Place the molasses in a saucepan. To this, add shortening, salt, soda and ginger. Stir well and bring to a boil. Remove from stovetop and allow the mixture to cool. When cooled to room temperature, start adding the flour, ½ cup at a time, until the mixture is at a consistency that will roll out very thin. (The batter will be non-sticky and stiff when enough flour has been added.) Cut out the cookies on a floured board by using a biscuit cutter or the rim of a juice glass. Bake in a 400-degree oven for 8 to 10 minutes or until done. Makes five to six dozen gingersnaps.

* I have no magic measurement for this one so I'll leave it up to you to decide "the size of an egg." When I make these cookies I usually use a *generous* heaping tablespoonful of shortening and that seems to work just fine.

Maly Rosol (Jelly-Filled Cookie)

Following are two cookie recipes that are flaky, delicate and delicious. They're typical Czech recipes because they believed in fillings.

½ lb. butter
2 cups flour
2 eggs
¼ tsp. salt
½ pt. sour cream
Cherry, blackberry, raspberry or apricot preserves
1 beaten egg
Few drops of vanilla
Confectioner's sugar

Rub butter and flour between hands into large bowl. Make a well in the center of the dough. Add two eggs, salt and sour cream. Work into smooth dough, or you may prefer to use your food processor. Divide the dough in half, wrap each section in plastic wrap and chill overnight. (Sugar is not missing, it's not added because the confectioners sugar on the floured board will work its way into the dough and sweeten it nicely. This dough will keep in the refrigerator for up to two weeks.)

Roll out on a board floured with confectioner's sugar. Cut into small squares. Fill the center of each square with a small amount of preserves. Fold and pinch the opposite corners together. Brush tops with beaten egg into which you've poured a couple drops of vanilla. Bake on greased sheet at 350 degrees for 25 minutes. Remove from pan immediately. When slightly cool, sprinkle with confectioner's sugar. Makes about 50 cookies.

Note: Your saving grace will be in using a silicone sheet mat because no matter how hard you try to seal the edges, the preserves will find a way to escape making cleanup more difficult.

Czechoslovakian Cookies

½ lb. butter, softened
1 cup sugar
2 egg yolks
2 cups flour
1 cup chopped walnuts or pecans
½ cup strawberry jam

Cream the butter and sugar together thoroughly. Add egg yolks; blend well. Gradually add flour; mix thoroughly. Add chopped nuts. Spoon half of mixture into a well-greased 8-inch square baking pan, spreading evenly. Top with jam; cover with the remaining batter. Bake at 325 degrees for 30 minutes or until lightly browned. Cool and cut into 1 x 2 inch squares. Makes 2 ½ dozen.

Hand-Cranked Homemade Ice Cream

When homemade ice cream was made at Grandma's, which was nearly every Sunday during the summer, a basic vanilla ice cream was made to which they usually added fresh peaches or strawberries just before it was ready to take out of the old hand-cranked freezer. Usually the job of cranking the handle fell to the men in the family because that was one thing around the kitchen that they were responsible for.

I remember watching my dad and uncles take hammers to smash the ice blocks until the ice broke off into little pieces, small enough to pack between the ice cream maker and the canister full of the wonderful rich custard. As they packed in the ice, they would layer it with salt, then ice, then more salt, until the freezer was full. They would then put newspapers over the whole bucket and start cranking. If it was a real hot day, they'd put an old blanket over the whole thing as well to keep it as cold as possible.

As the original ice melted, more was added. Although I don't think it took too terribly long for the ice cream to form, it seemed like it took forever. We were told many times to "go play, we'll let you know when it's ready." And they did.

1 quart of milk
1 quart of cream
2 cups of sugar
2 eggs
1 tsp. vanilla

Place on ice until thoroughly cold. Pour into ice cream canister, secure lid and assemble the ice cream maker.

Note: We have learned that raw eggs may carry harmful bacteria so unfortunately it is no longer advisable to use them in uncooked recipes. My advice is to put the well-mixed ingredients into a saucepan and slowly bring them up to 160 degrees. After reaching the recommended temperature, remove from stove, allow to cool, then refrigerate until ready to pack into the canister.

Gingerbread

Aunt Margaret seemed happy to let me cook with her whenever I wanted to during my visits to the farm. Once she handed me a cookbook and told me to bake something. I chose to make gingerbread and was so proud when even the boys told me how good it was. I don't have that recipe today, but this is an old-fashioned recipe that I use when I make it now.

2/3 cup of boiling water
1/3 cup of shortening
1 cup molasses
1 egg
2 ¾ cup flour
2 tsp. soda
1 tsp. cinnamon
1 ½ tsp. ginger
¼ tsp. cloves

Melt shortening in boiling water. Add molasses and beaten egg. Add dry ingredients and blend. Bake in a greased pan at 350 degrees for 30 minutes.

Angel Food Cake

So many Czech recipes call for the use of egg yolks in baking leaving us with egg whites on our hands. Using them in an angle food cake recipe is an easy and frugal way to use the whites. This cake is really good. It could be doubled and put into a tube pan as well.

¾ cup sifted flour
¼ cup cornstarch
1 cup egg whites
½ tsp. salt
¼ tsp almond extract

1 tsp. cream of tartar
1 ¼ cups sugar
¾ tsp. vanilla

Sift flour several times. Set aside. Beat egg whites and salt until foamy. Add cream of tartar and continue beating whites until they are stiff enough to hold up in peaks. Carefully fold in sugar, adding only a small amount at a time.

Once the sugar is incorporated into the whites, follow by folding in the flour. Do not overmix. Add seasonings.

Pour batter into ungreased loaf pan and bake at least one hour in a slow oven. (Begin at 275 degrees and, after 30 minutes, increase to 325 degrees.) Remove from oven and invert pan for one hour, or until cake is cold. Remove from pan.

Plain Cake

Back in the early days, our family rarely made decorated or fancy cakes and if my mom ever used a cake recipe, I never saw it. Fancy cakes were made on special occasions like holidays and birthdays. Other times, cakes were made simply with maybe a glaze or powdered sugar frosting with some cocoa added if we wanted chocolate.

I believe Mom, like the others, made cakes so often that it was ingrained into her head. She also never used a measuring cup or measuring spoon as I can remember. Rather she'd pour the flour and sugar right out of the canisters or bags that they came in right into her mixing bowl. She'd reach in the drawer and take out a teaspoon or soup spoon to measure the other dry ingredients while pouring the extracts right out of the bottle. To mix everything together, I did see her use her eggbeater once in a while.

The best part of it all was, if we begged hard enough she let us eat it warm, as soon as the cake came out of the oven, unfrosted, we did not care. This was the time before TV, when we were all gathered around the radio listening to our favorite shows, and the smell of that cake baking was more than we could stand. I guess we got on Mom's nerves long enough for her to give in and give us a big piece, just to shut us up. Not always, but sometimes.

½ cupful of butter or other shortening
1 cupful sugar
2 eggs
2 cups flour
3 tsp. baking powder
¼ cup of milk
1 ½ teaspoonfuls of vanilla

Cream the butter well and stir in the sugar gradually. Beat the egg and stir into the creamed butter and the sugar. Mix and sift the flour and the baking powder together and add alternately with the milk, beating well between each addition. Flavor and pour into two 9-inch layer-cake pans. Bake at 375 degrees 25 to 30 minutes. Frost when cool.

I call this small cake "anything can be added cake" because to make it coconut, add ¼ cup coconut to the batter and ¾ cup pressed into the icing. To make it chocolate, add chocolate, to make it pineapple, add drained crushed pineapple between the layers. You get the picture. It's a great cake to be creative with.

Grandma's Birthday Cake

My grandma, Christina, was born on September 6, 1881. She was not yet two years old when she came to America and the story goes that she learned to walk while on board the ship making the crossing. Every year to celebrate her birthday, Aunt Margaret would make this wonderful three-layer cake. Not one crumb was ever left on the cake plate because it was so good. But delicious as it is, every time anyone makes it, they never fail to preface it with this sentence: "This cake certainly is not a pretty one, but it sure is delicious."

I'm not sure of the real name of this cake but I think it's an old recipe called the "Surprise Cake." I believe that is what Aunt Margaret told me once and it's very likely because of the center layer. It really doesn't matter because it has been renamed "Grandma's Birthday Cake" by everyone I know who makes it. Nancy Cerny Edwards, my cousin, and Rae Blaha, my sister-in-law, make this cake better than anyone I know. They are willing to take theirs to special events—mine however, never looks good enough to take out in public.

The cake consists of three layers, two yellow sponge cake layers and one angel food cake layer. This cake is topped with an awesome caramel icing that must be watched while cooking because if cooked too long, it can quickly become too hard to spread.

1st and 3rd Yellow Cake layers
5 eggs, separated (reserve whites for middle layer)
1 cup sugar
½ cup milk
1 ¼ cup flour
1 tsp. salt
1 tsp. soda
1 tsp. cream of tartar
½ tsp. vanilla

Beat egg yolks and sugar until lemon in color. Add milk and vanilla. Mix dry ingredients together and gently fold into the egg mixture. Bake in two pans at 350 degrees for about 20 minutes.

Middle Angel Food Cake layer
5 egg whites
Pinch of salt
¾ tsp. cream of tartar
¾ cup sugar
1 tsp. vanilla
½ cup flour

Beat egg whites until soft peaks form. Gradually add sugar, cream of tartar and salt until stiff peaks form. Fold in flour. Add vanilla. Bake in one pan for 20 minutes at 325 degrees. Do not overcook.

Frosting
1 box light brown sugar
1 ½ cups light cream or 1 ½ cup milk plus 1 tablespoon of butter (do not use canned milk)
1 tsp. vanilla

Mix together the sugar and cream. Bring to a boil over medium heat and boil until it reaches a soft boil stage. Stir occasionally. At the soft ball stage remove from the heat and let cool. Add vanilla and beat until it reaches a spreading consistency.

Tip: Before frosting the cake, place torn strips of waxed paper on the cake plate under the bottom layer of the cake to catch the icing as it drips down the sides. Pull the strips of paper away when the cake has been frosted, but before the frosting has hardened.

This recipe, as several of the others in this book, was told to us verbally and usually written down on whatever paper was handy or on the back of an old envelope. Now that we all have timers, candy thermometers, and no longer have to pull straws out of our brooms to use as cake testers, it is easier to get good results. Personally I wouldn't even try to make this recipe without these aids anymore. It was suggested once to use yellow and angel food cake mixes in this recipe, and while I'm sure it would work, a good Bohemian cook would never do that, even though it would definitely make a prettier cake.

Baking Bread in Gernik, 2006, photo courtesy of Joyce Pritchard

An Old Country Easter Tradition

Most religions and believers celebrate springtime as a symbol of New Life. In their traditional way they too celebrate it by honoring their own age-old customs. Here is one way most Bohemians honored their Christianity at Eastertime.

Easter was only second to Christmas as far as important holidays in the old country. For Czechoslovakians, Eastertime had important symbolic meanings. Though it is no longer customary today, in the past, Bohemians put together a decorated wicker basket full of symbolic food and took it to church on the eve before Easter to have it blessed by the priest. They believed that these blessings early in the new spring would help them through the year ahead. The lamb, sometimes molded in butter and decorated with a small cross, represented the goodness of Christ that we should have for each other. Beautifully decorated eggs adorned the basket and represented a new life and Christ's resurrection. Ham symbolized great joy and abundance, while sausage, God's favor and generosity. Salt is to remind us of our Christian duty to others and horseradish mixed with grated red beets was symbolic of the Passion of Christ still with us. Sugar added, is His resurrection, and all of it being bittersweet reminds us of His suffering. Butter and cheese represented the goodness of Christ and of the moderation Christians should have of all things. The Easter Bread, Butcha (Czech) Pascha (Slovak) is symbolic of Christ Himself, the giver of life; the plait his crown. This Easter bread was usually wrapped separately and covered by a large linen cloth embroidered with the words "Christ is Risen." A candle was placed in this basket among the food and was lit at the time of the blessing. No one ate until after they had received communion on Easter Sunday. Then they would break their fast. (Breakfast!)

These beautiful traditions are centuries old and unfortunately they seem to have been diluted throughout time, having lost their original meanings. What better way to change that than by keeping alive some of the old traditions and customs that were honored and celebrated by our ancestors.

Although many of us make an Easter lamb cake for the "kids" at Easter, I wonder how many of us think about how and why this tradition originated in our families?

Easter Lamb Cake

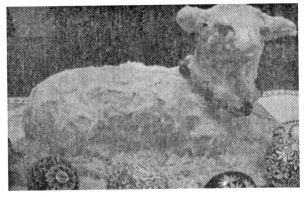

A basic pound cake recipe should always be used in making this cake when baked in a mold. Other cakes are just too light to hold up to the handling it requires. Children love to help decorate this cake and it's a delight to watch them take part in this tradition.

2 cups butter
2 ¼ cups sugar
8 eggs (2 cups)
5 cups sifted cake flour
½ tsp. salt
1 tsp. vanilla
Lamb mold

Beat butter and sugar until light and fluffy. Add eggs one at a time, beating well after each addition. Sift the dry ingredients together and add to creamed mixture. Add vanilla and mix only until blended. Pour into a *very well greased and floured* lamb mold, pouring the batter into the face side only. Before baking, carefully insert two or three toothpicks into the wet cake mixture at the neck of the mold to stabilize this weak area. Cover the cake mixture with the back side of the lamb mold and bake about 50 minutes. Remove from oven and cool on rack about 25–30 minutes before removing from mold.

Place cake on top of a bed of coconut (grass) that has been tinted with green food coloring. (To tint coconut, place it into a glass jar, add a few drops of food coloring. Cover jar tightly and shake until thoroughly coated.) Frost with a fluffy white icing and use jelly beans to make the eyes and necklace.

Fluffy White Frosting
2 ¼ cup confectioners sugar
1 stick butter, softened
1 tsp. vanilla
Water

Mix sugar, butter and vanilla together until well blended. If icing is too thick add 1 teaspoon of water at a time until it is soft and fluffy. Spread icing over lamb cake, making soft swirls and peaks to resemble lamb's wool.

Old Bohemian Traditional Bread and Pastries

Babka (Baba or Babovka)

In the old country this is the bread that traditionally was prepared on the Saturday before Easter and taken along with other symbolic foods to church to be blessed, then eaten the next day at the Easter feast. It is light and rich in color and texture and makes a beautiful presentation. When I think how this bread is made, I have a new appreciation for our ancestors who made this recipe generations ago and who did not have modern kitchen tools and equipment to work with as we have now. For instance, I can't imagine working the melted butter into the dough by hand. Although 15 egg yolks sounds extensive to us today, back then on their farms, eggs were plentiful and it was not at all unusual to use that many in bread and cake recipes like it is today.

Making babka is personally satisfying. It is an accomplishment because the outcome makes such a stunning presentation. Recently, I offered a slice to a friend and the first bite stopped her in her tracks—she closed her eyes, stopped chewing and was finally able to tell me that with just that one bite, it took her back home to her mother's kitchen. She asked for the recipe that I gladly gave her.

In Polish custom, this cake-like bread is known as grandmother's cake because it resembled her skirts. It is an honored recipe and if you ever want to show off your baking culinary skills, this is the one to do it with. There are special baking pans for babka, but a regular fluted tube cake pan works also.

1 ¼ cups milk
4 to 5 cups flour
2 yeast cakes
½ cup plus 1 Tbsp. sugar
15 egg yolks
¼ tsp. salt
½ tsp. vanilla extract
¼ tsp. almond extract
½ cup melted butter

Scald milk. Put 1 cup of milk in mixing bow. Add ¾ cup flour to milk. Stir until smooth. Allow the remaining ¼ cup milk to cool. When lukewarm, add 1 tablespoon sugar to the yeast cakes that have been crumbled. Add the flour and yeast mixtures together. Cover and set aside.

Beat egg yolks with salt and remaining ½ cup sugar until mixture is thick and lemon-colored. When the yeast sponge is bubbling, add egg mixture. Beat well. Add remaining flour and extracts. Work until dough is satin smooth. Add melted butter and knead until the butter is worked in. Cover. Let rise until doubled in bulk. Punch down and cover to rise again. Put on floured board and knead well. Put into well-buttered babka pans or fluted tube cake pans.

Mix a little sugar and melted butter with the scraps of dough left in the bowl and sprinkle these rich crumbs over the top of the babka. Let the babka rise until light. Bake for approximately 50 minutes in an oven preheated to 350 degrees.

Pagaèky
(Biscuits with Cracklings)

My father was the breakfast cook in our house when I was growing up. As a tugboat captain he hauled sand and gravel up the James River to Richmond, Virginia, each night, so that it would be in port each morning for the dock workers to unload. Dad would usually return home early in the morning just about the time to wake us up for school. He may have already cooked the sausage or bacon and put the biscuits in the oven, waiting for us to gather before he cooked the eggs.

Traditionally at hog-killing time, those who went out to the farm to help butcher were rewarded with a crock full of raw pork that had been stuffed in lard to preserve it, along with a fat package of delicious cracklings to take home with them, and some of Grandpa's sausage. His father made two of the best sausages I ever tasted and I rue the day that I did not ask for his recipes.

Usually the cracklings and sausages were saved and cooked at special times because we did not get it but once a year. It was a real treat when we had some of Grandpa's sausage on our breakfast table. As children we were never taken to the farm during "that" time and it was a long time before I learned that cracklings were actually fried (rendered) pork skins. By that time I didn't care, they were so delicious. Often instead of adding them to biscuits, Dad would scramble them in eggs. Either way, we loved them and his wonderful breakfasts.

3 cups flour
½ cup sugar
3 tsp. baking powder
1 tsp. salt
2 cups cracklings, finely ground
2 eggs
½ cup milk or more to make soft dough

Mix flour with cracklings until well blended. Add rest of ingredients and mix well. Form into patties and place on buttered cookie sheet. Bake at 350 degrees for about 20 minutes.

Sweet Braided Bread (Buchta/Vanocka)

My cousin Nancy Cerny Edwards gave me her recipe for this wonderful bread. When we were neighbors, she would bring me a loaf every Christmas. Her notes stated: "Beautiful, delicious sweet bread for anytime, but especially for holidays. For some reason we always called it Christmas Bread. But don't save it for only that season."

Ingredients:
3 cups all-purpose flour (approximately)
¼ cup sugar
2 eggs (beaten)
¼ cup unsalted butter (softened)
½ tsp. salt
¼ cup lukewarm milk
1 package active dry yeast
¼ cup warm water (105–115 degrees)
½ cup English walnuts
½ cup raisins
1 tsp. orange peel
1 tsp. lemon peel

In a large mixing bowl, dissolve yeast in warm water, let stand approximately 10 minutes. Meanwhile, heat milk but do not boil. Stir in sugar, butter, salt, orange and lemon rinds, mixing together until dissolved. Add approximately 1 cup of flour to yeast mixture. Allow this mixture to form a sponge-like texture. Next, add beaten eggs, mixing well. Stir in walnuts and raisins. Begin adding more flour until a good dough consistency is achieved. Knead on floured surface until smooth and elastic. Place dough in greased bowl, greased side up, and allow to stand covered until it doubles in size. When dough has risen, punch down and begin assembling three separate braids.

To make the braids, pull a small amount of dough and roll between your palms to make a strip, (each braid requires three strips); criss-cross the strips to braid. Set aside—do this twice more. Lay two braided strips side-by-side on your baking sheet; lay the third braid on top and in the center of the two bottom strips, forming the loaf. Set aside to rise. Bake at 350 degrees for about 45 minutes until golden brown. Remove from oven and rub with butter.

Nancy added a note which read, "We have somewhat modernized this by using Hot Roll Mix, which comes with yeast. You will still need some flour for consistency."

Walnut Bread

My sister, Patty, has become the family expert in making this recipe. It tastes, looks, and feels like a cake, but it's a bread. It is wonderful and will keep for weeks, especially when a good red wine is poured over it and then wrapped tightly. Freezing it is another alternative. Mom used to set aside one whole day to make this bread every Thanksgiving and Christmas. Now Patty has taken over making it for our family and her friends.

Mama's recipe was written down in one of her cookbooks with a great list of ingredients, but the directions were written only as her notes. It took Patty and me some time to re-write her instructions. She assumed we had seen her and helped her do it enough that her notes were all that we needed. Here is what she wrote: "Mix bread dough and shortening well (low speed). Add eggs, sugar, wine and soda. (Put your soda in the wine to dissolve.) Mix all other ingredients. Let rise I hour and bake at 325 for 1 hour or longer." Patty's directions given here are much easier than Mom's.

Assemble all of the ingredients together. Set aside.

Make bread dough using your favorite recipe or the one given in this recipe. Set aside.

Mix wine and soda together. Set aside.

Sift together 2 cups flour with nutmeg and cinnamon. Set aside.

1 ½ cups prepared bread dough (see recipe below)
1 cup shortening
4 eggs
2 cups sugar
1 ½ cups water
½ cup red wine
1 tsp. soda
1 tsp. nutmeg
1 tsp. cinnamon
1 cup raisins
1 cup black walnuts

To make the bread dough:

1 package dry yeast dissolved in ¼ cup water
2 cups milk (scalded)
½ cup melted butter
2 Tbsp. sugar
2 tsp. salt
6 cups all-purpose flour

Pour hot milk over butter to melt. Add sugar and salt. Cool to lukewarm and add yeast and 3 cups of flour. Beat well and add remaining flour. Knead until smooth and satiny. One and one-half cups of this dough is needed for each walnut bread that is made.

(The remaining dough could be used to make loaves of white bread. If so, allow it to rise until double in bulk. Punch down; form into loaves, place in greased and floured loaf pans and let rise for 30 minutes. Bake in hot oven, 400 degrees for 35 minutes.)

Step 1. Using an electric mixer with a dough hook and on slow speed, incorporate the shortening into the prepared bread dough. This will break the dough down. Once the dough and shortening have been mixed together, add the eggs and sugar, along with the wine/soda mixture. Beat until all is well incorporated.

Step 2. To this mixture, add flour and spices alternately with the water. Continue mixing until batter is well incorporated.

Step 3. Fold in black walnuts and raisins that have been coated with flour.

Step 4. Place batter into a well-greased tube cake pan. Let rise 1 hour then bake at 325 degrees for 1 hour. Test, using a cake tester to make sure the center is done. When partially cool, take the bread out of the pan and place it on a rack to cool.

After the walnut bread has cooled if not to be served right away, pick holes into the top of the cake and pour red wine over the entire surface. Wrap in cheesecloth then foil. Soaked and wrapped in this manner, this bread will keep for several weeks without freezing. If it is to be kept longer, wrap tightly and freeze.

All About Making Peanut Rolls, Kolaches and Strudel

Until I traveled to Europe and visited the large markets in Budapest, it never occurred to me that the delicious peanut rolls our family made all these years were actually take-offs of the famous European nut and poppy seed rolls so popular in Slavic countries.

We discovered these delicious little loaves in the markets in Budapest, not only in bake shops, but also in unlikely places—hidden among sausages, paprika, salami and other delicate pastries in various food stalls. These markets were astonishing and we visited them daily while in this captivating city. Although on our last trip to the markets before returning home, I purchased two nut rolls to bring back with me, only one survived. We couldn't resist delving into one of them during some of the long waits we had in the various airplane terminals between flights back home.

The nut rolls my grandma made were larger and shaped differently than the European ones. Grandma's were fatter, longer and before being baked, formed into a slight crescent. Once sliced the spirals made a beautiful presentation. It finally occurred to me that because our grandparents grew peanuts on their farm and they were so abundant, Grandma used them as her version of these delicious nut rolls.

Grandma could have used pecans as well as peanuts because they had several large trees growing right next to the house, but she used them in fruitcakes, cookies, and in other ways, rather than in nut rolls. As delicious as European nut rolls are, roasted peanuts give a distinctly different taste and in my opinion, greatly improves the flavor.

Dough for Peanut Rolls and Kolaches

The dough recipe for making the dough used for peanut rolls is the same as the dough for making Kolaches. None of the ladies in our family has ever used any other recipe because this one gives such wonderful results. It is easy to make and results in a soft, pliable, easy-to-manage dough that is both beautiful and delicious. To make kolaches, small pieces of dough are pulled off and made into rolls that will eventually hold various fillings. If making peanut rolls, it is rolled out thin, filled with a nut or poppy seed filling and rolled up to be baked. Either way it's used, it's a pleasure to work with this dough recipe.

Peanut Rolls

1 cup scalded milk
½ cup sugar
½ cup butter
1 yeast cake or 1 package dry yeast
¼ cup warm water
1 egg
¾ tsp. salt
4 to 5 cups all-purpose flour

Scald milk. Remove from heat, add sugar and butter; stir, allowing them to melt while cooling. Set aside. Dissolve yeast in ¼ cup warm water. Set aside. Add salt to 4 cups of flour. Set aside.

In a large mixing bowl, add the egg and yeast to the milk mixture. Slowly add the dry ingredients to the wet mixture. Add more flour as needed.

Turn the dough out on a floured surface and knead about 10 minutes or until the dough is soft, pliable and elastic. (A mixer with a dough hook attached may be used.) Place in lightly greased bowl, cover, and let rise until doubled in size.

When the dough has risen and doubled its size, remove it to a lightly floured surface and punch it down to remove the air. Divide the dough in half and working half of the dough at a time, roll it out into thin rectangles about 1/8 inch thick—ready to spread with the filling or if using for kolaches, squeeze out small balls of dough as if making hot rolls, place on a greased pan and let rise once again. When risen the second time, make a depression in the center of each roll and fill with your favorite fruit or poppy seed filling.

Peanut Roll Filling

1 cup raw peanuts, finely chopped
1 cup sugar
2 Tbsp. cinnamon
1 stick butter, melted

Using a food processor, mix all ingredients together. When evenly mixed, spread the filling on the rectangles of dough and roll tightly in a jellyroll fashion. Seal the long end by pinching the seam together tightly using a little water on one edge. Next push each end of the roll back into the center of the log to seal. Place on a greased baking sheet or silicone mat. Loaf pans may also be used if preferred. Let the rolls rise a second time before baking. If desired, brush the peanut rolls with an egg wash made by adding a little vanilla to a beaten egg. Bake at 350 degrees for 30–35 minutes, somewhat longer if loaf pans are used. Remove from pans and place on racks to cool.

(Mom always tapped the rolls listening for a "hollow sound" which she claimed indicated the rolls were done and ready to come out of the oven. To this day, I still do this little ritual even though I'm not sure that it's the best way to tell if they're done.)

Kolaches

Preheat oven to 425 degrees.
1 batch of dough used for Peanut Rolls
Filling of your choice (see following suggestions)

After the first rising of this dough, squeeze out small balls of dough as if making hot rolls, place on a greased pan and let rise once again. When risen the second time, make a depression in the center of each roll and fill with your favorite fruit or poppy seed filling. Leave room between rolls so they can brown evenly on all sides. Bake 10 to 12 minutes. Brush with melted butter and remove to racks to cool.

Tip: If one is in a hurry, frozen rolls could be thawed and used. Just remember that the older generations of Czechs and Slovaks will not think of them as authentic homemade kolaches.

Whole Poppy Seed Filling

Poppy seed was bought whole in the past and it had to be ground, sweetened and boiled long enough to soften the hard outer shell and to bring out the nutty flavor. Poppy seed grinders can still be found, but they can also be ground in a home coffee grinder. It is no longer necessary to grind poppy seeds as they can be bought in a can already prepared and ready to serve. They are also available in food stores already ground, to be sprinkled in recipes. For kolaches, I strongly recommend buying the already prepared poppy seed as it's a lot less work, is just as good and just as cheap. For anyone who wishes to do it the old way here is our recipe.

1 lb. poppy seed
2 cups sugar
1 egg
Sweet cream

Grind poppy seed. Add sugar, egg and sweet cream to make a paste. Bring mixture to a boil and allow it to boil about 5 minutes. Remove from heat and cover allowing it to stand undisturbed for about an hour. Using about 1 tablespoon of the mixture, fill the depressions in the dough that has been prepared for kolaches. Bake 12–15 minutes at 425 degrees. Remember, canned poppy seed is available in most grocery stores. Add a little sugar to it and one will never know the difference unless you tell them.

Two Cheese Filling

1 (8 oz.) pkg. cream cheese, softened
1 (8 oz.) container cottage cheese
1 cup sugar
1 Tbsp. flour
1 egg yolk
¼ tsp. lemon juice

Combine all ingredients together and mix well. Using about 1 tablespoon of the mixture, fill depressions in the dough and bake 12–15 minutes at 425 degrees. This recipe makes enough to fill about four dozen kolaches.

Fruit Fillings

Czechs seem to prefer apple, prune or cherry as fruit fillings when making kolaches. Made with either fresh or dried fruits, prepare it as you would for your favorite pie, i.e., peel and chop, add sugar and spices (usually cinnamon) then cook until tender. Fill the kolaches and bake 12–15 minutes at 425 degrees.

Tip: A good brand of fruit preserves or "spiced up" applesauce are also options as Kolache fillings. Just don't mention that you used preserves instead of making the fruit from scratch. The "Senior" Bohemians do not claim these time-savers as genuine.

Nut or Poppy Seed Strudel

To use the pecans that we gathered on the farm, and later those my grandson Johnathan picked up at his house for me, here is a wonderful recipe that is very similar to the nut rolls we bought in Budapest. They turn out beautifully and taste wonderful. These freeze very well if made ahead.

4 cups flour
½ cup sugar
1 tsp. salt
1 package dry yeast
1 cup milk
¼ cup water
1 egg
½ cup butter

In a large bowl mix 1¼ cup flour, sugar, salt and undissolved dry yeast. Combine milk, water and butter in a saucepan. Heat slowly to lukewarm. Remove from heat. Add egg and ¾ cup flour to make a thick batter. Let sit until it reaches a sponge-like consistency. Stir in the rest of the flour making a stiff dough. Cover with foil. Refrigerate at least 2 hours or it may be kept for up to 3 days.

Divide dough in half on floured board. Roll each section into a 14x7-inch rectangle. Spread with nut or poppy seed filling. Roll up and place on a greased pan. Let rise until double in size. Bake at 375 degrees for 20–25 minutes. Remove to racks to cool before slicing. Makes 2 nut rolls.

Easy Poppy Seed Filling

1 can poppy seed
Sugar to taste
Combine sugar and poppy seed. Mix well. Spread on prepared, rolled-out dough. Roll up and seal all edges.

Nut Filling

1 ½ lb. pecans (walnuts may be substituted)
1 cup sugar
¾ cup brown sugar
1 Tbsp. cinnamon
Soft butter
½ stick soft butter

Spread dough with butter. Sprinkle the dough with nuts, the two sugars and cinnamon. Roll tightly; seal all edges.

The Old Country

The rustic outside kitchen used to cook for the crowds at the Gernik festival.

Eating in a remote foreign country is somewhat threatening because seldom do we know what to expect. In the village, during our visit, we were ecstatic to find that the food they served us was exactly as we remembered it to be, in other words, just like Mom's. For those of us who have Czech and Slovak ancestors, eating a meal in the village was like going back in time and pulling up a chair to the kitchen table. It was like going home. It was familiar, fresh, and delicious. Our ethnic recipes and ways of cooking them that we learned from the old folks were justified as the dishes we make tasted very much like those we ate while there. For non-Czechs in our group it was just "unusual."

We noticed that in Gernik, families baked their bread daily. Further, they grow all of their own vegetables, grain, and raise all of their meat products. We had forgotten that soup was always served as a first course for lunch and dinner, and that it was almost always a chicken-based soup. And their kolaches, oh my goodness, they were the size of a dinner plate compared to those we make, ours being the size of a dinner roll. They were delicious, filled with fruit or poppy seed fillings, just like we do at home.

Another surprise for some in our group who had never eaten European breakfasts was that it consisted of sausages, cold cuts, fresh vegetables and cheese. Not the typical eggs and bacon, cold cereals and milk that we normally eat at home.

We found that it was really difficult for most of us to eat all the food we were served, as delicious as it was. Even more difficult for us was to reject it, to leave food on our plates, as we didn't want to seem ungrateful or wasteful.

The way we managed this was that we learned to take very small portions and to eat everything that we put on our plates and to drink everything that we accepted, including their famous homemade brandy, slivovitz. One shot of this strong liquor was the most that any of us could handle, as it is very potent. They are proud of their homemade plum brandy and use any occasion to have a celebratory salute. We soon realized (some the hard way) that "toasts" were just as wonderful with soda as with their slivovitz.

We were so fortunate to be in the village during their Folk Festival, held every two years. Music and dance and costumes from all over the region were on display during that entire festive weekend. What a blessing it was for all of us to have had this opportunity, to meet our foreign relatives was enough, but to see and experience their way of life and their daily living; to hear and see their customs, their music, dance, and food preparations, to interact with them in different ways and to see and experience the joy and fellowship as we did, was for all of us, a lifetime experience that we'll never forget.

The Village Festivities

Our teenage granddaughter, Shelly Pearson, who traveled to the village with us, made a striking contrast as she stood next to the village teens who were dressed in their beautiful folk dresses. They formed a mutual admiration society as seen in their glances and smiles to each other.

Honoring our Bohemian Heritage

The remote Czech village of Gernik, our family village, now in Romania, is where many ancestors of Southern Virginians emigrated to from Bohemia about 1826. During the late 1890s, some fifty years later, some of our relatives left this little village for America to settle in the Virginia counties of Dinwiddie, Prince George, Chesterfield, and Greensville where these little farming colonies continue to exist.

Today, five generations later, some of the original farms are still in the same families, still viable and productive, having incorporated new technology, modern farming techniques and equipment as it became available during the past 100 years. Not only that, and perhaps even more remarkable is that these same Bohemian families continue to worship in the 100-year-old churches that were built by their ancestors when they established their little farming communities in Southern Virginia. Remarkably, these old Bohemian families, through these five generations, have continued to maintain and carry forth friendships and interactions among them, that began over 150 years ago in their native Bohemian village of Gernik.

A Note from the Author

The Blaha Family in Gernik, RO

When we met our relatives in Gernik for the first time ever, we were all in awe of this event. None of us ever dreamed that this would be possible due to time and distance and global circumstances. There was a mystical feeling in the air that somehow as we looked at each other, we knew we belonged, and a warm sense of family and friendship prevailed.

It would have been impossible to communicate with each other without the help of our gracious interpreters, Dr. Dzenek Uherik, a professor of ethnology at Charles University in Prague, and Daniel Mair, a former American scholar at the university, now living in Prague. By serving as our interpreters we were able to acknowledge and to share a little about each other—enough for them to know that their relatives in the United States cared enough to find them in their little corner of the world and to share what we could with them about our way of life here. This first visit to our ancestral village, this first look at a way of life that our immigrant forefathers brought to America with them, gave us new insights. The ability to take a glance back at our own heritage was truly a once-in-a-lifetime experience for us, and to be honest a life-changing one as well. It was truly a joyful event and one that will forever remain in our hearts.

About the Author

Marie Blaha Pearson is the cofounder of the Southside Virginia Czech Slovak Heritage Society with interests in retaining the history, customs and traditions of the former Czechoslovakia. Her love of cooking and collecting recipes began as a child on her immigrant grandparents' farm and has continued during her fifty years of homemaking.

In 1998 Marie's first visit to the Czech Republic was with a church mission. She returned twice more, once to find and visit the ancestral village of her immigrant grandparents in 2005, then in 2006, she was invited to present a paper, "Exploring Czech Families of Immigrants, 100 Years Later..." at the World Congress of the Czechoslovak Society of Arts and Sciences (SVU) held at the University of Southern Bohemia in Ceske Budejovice.

Marie is a summa cum laude graduate of St. Leo University. Before her retirement she was the director of Virginia Osteoporosis Clinic.